SUCCESS AND SUSTAINABILITY INDICATORS

SUCCESS and SUSTAINABILITY INDICATORS

— a tool to assess primary collection schemes

Case study: Khulna, Bangladesh

*Jenny Appleton, Mansoor Ali
and Andrew Cotton*

Water, Engineering and Development Centre
Loughborough University
2000

Water, Engineering and Development Centre,
Loughborough University,
Leicestershire, LE11 3TU, UK

© WEDC, Loughborough University, 2000

ISBN 13 Paperback: 978 0 90605 573 1
ISBN Ebook: 9781788533591
Book DOI: http://dx.doi.org/10.3362/9781788533591

A catalogue record for this book is available from the British Library.

A reference copy of this publication is also available online at:
http://www.lboro.ac.uk/wedc/publications/

Appleton, J., Ali, M. and Cotton, A. (2000)
Success and Sustainability Indicators:
A Tool to Assess Primary Collection Schemes: A Case Study of Khulna, Bangladesh,
WEDC, Loughborough University, UK.

WEDC (The Water, Engineering and Development Centre) at Loughborough University in the UK is one of the world's leading institutions concerned with education, training, research and consultancy for the planning, provision and management of physical infrastructure for development in low- and middleincome countries.

This edition is reprinted and distributed by Practical Action Publishing.
Since 1974, Practical Action Publishing has published and disseminated books and information in support of international development work throughout the world. Practical Action Publishing trades only in support of its parent charity objectives and any profits are covenanted back to Practical Action (Charity Reg. No. 247257, Group VAT Registration No. 880 9924 76).

This document is an output from a project funded by the UK
Department for International Development (DFID)
for the benefit of low-income countries.
The views expressed are not necessarily those of DFID.

Designed at WEDC

About the Authors

Jenny Appleton is a Research Assistant at WEDC. She graduated from the University of Nottingham with an MEng in Civil Engineering in 1999 and has since been working at WEDC, mainly in the field of solid waste management. She undertook the fieldwork for this study during a period spent in Bangladesh working with the Water and Sanitation Group, South Asia, Bangladesh.

Dr Mansoor Ali is a Project/Programme Manager at WEDC. A specialist in solid waste management for low-income countries, he has researched and published extensively on the subject and is currently involved with the research projects *Capacity Building, Micro-enterprise Development* and *Appropriate Landfilling.*

Dr Andrew Cotton is the Director of Urban Programmes WEDC. A specialist in urban infrastructure for low-income countries, some of his recent research includes micro-contrasts, operation and maintenance, knowledge management and urban sanitation.

Acknowledgements

The following persons made valuable contributions to this research:

Local Collaborators

Dr Babar Kabir	Water and Sanitation Group, South Asia, Bangladesh
Dr Tanveer Ahsan	Water and Sanitation Group, South Asia, Bangladesh
Shafiul Azam Ahmad	Water and Sanitation Group, South Asia, Bangladesh
Monir Alam Chowdhury	Prodipan, Bangladesh

Others

Rod Shaw	WEDC, UK
Marielle Snel	WEDC, UK
Jon Rouse	Freelance Consultant

Contents

List of Tables

Figure

Acronyms

NGO   Non-Governmental Organisation

CBO   Community Based Organisation

KCC   Khulna City Corporation

Tk   Taka, currency of Bangladesh (1 US\$ $\approx$ Tk50 in 2000)

Glossary

Demountable containers	Moveable containers used to collect waste
Eid	Islamic festival
Sweepers	Street cleaners employed by the municipality
Ward	Administrative section of the city
Ward commissioner	Elected representative of the Ward

Introduction

A list of success and sustainability indicators for primary solid waste collection systems was prepared by the project team as part of the Knowledge and Research (KAR) research project, *Capacity Building for Primary Collection of Solid Waste*, funded by the UK Department for International Development (DFID). The indicators were prepared in an attempt to assist fieldworkers when undertaking impact assessments of primary solid waste collection schemes. Such assessments are frequently done from only one perspective and fail to take the views of all the major stakeholders into consideration. These indicators draw attention to the fact that the opinions of all stakeholders, including the urban poor, are relevant in assessing the success and sustainability of a project. They are developed around past studies of primary collection schemes based mainly in South Asia.

This booklet presents the indicators, their use and results from their field-testing. This field-testing was carried out in March 2000 in Khulna City, Bangladesh, in collaboration with the Water and Sanitation Programme (WSP), Dhaka, Bangladesh. The final section of the booklet draws lessons on further use of the indicators.

1.

Success and Sustainability Indicators for Primary Collection Schemes

1.1 Primary solid waste collection schemes: An overview

In urban areas, solid waste collection systems are normally provided by municipalities. In high-income developed countries, this usually entails the collection of waste from properties and its subsequent conveyance to a municipal disposal site. However, in most low-income countries, the door-to-door collection of waste is not provided, and it is normally the responsibility of the householder to convey their waste to a communal bin or transfer point provided in the locality. The municipality then collects the waste from these points and takes it to the final disposal site. However, the municipality is frequently under-staffed and under-financed, resulting in a poor service. Communal bins and transfer points are often too far away for the easy transfer of waste by householders. As a result, waste builds up in local areas, on streets and vacant plots presenting a hazard to the local residents. This is truer in low-income areas of cities than anywhere else. Primary solid waste collection schemes have been initiated in many low-income countries in response to this problem. These schemes are managed by NGOs, community groups, micro-contractors or local politicians. They provide the door-to-door collection of waste and its subsequent transportation to the local municipal bins. The service charges are usually made directly to the users of the service but sometimes supplemented by external funding. In most circumstances, the schemes develop as a result of a demand shown by the local residents and are paid for by the householders who receive the service.

1.2   Why do we need success and sustainability indicators?

When it comes to assessing the performance of primary solid waste collection schemes, there are very few tools available. One tool which can be developed is a list of indicators that will draw attention to the various aspects of each project which contribute in some way to the project's success or sustainability. This provides the fieldworker with a checklist against which to perform a detailed analysis of the project and provides a way of comparing the success and sustainability of different schemes.

The indicators are arranged in lists according to the group whose perspective is sought on each issue. If the indicators are considered from the perspective of one stakeholder only, they may disadvantage another group. It is important that the views of all major stakeholders in each scheme are considered carefully. This will also help each of the groups of major stakeholders to evaluate the present scheme and develop ways to improve it. The lists of indicators are presented in tables to reflect the different perspectives of the major stakeholders. Each table has the following three columns:

1. The indicator;

2. Its description; and,

3. How to measure the indicator.

It is important to realize that these indicators are country and area-specific, and priorities of certain indicators may be stronger in some places and at some times than others.

1.3 The indicators

1.3.1 The users' perspective

How do the users judge the scheme?

Table 1. The users' perspective		
Indicator	*Description*	*Means to measure*
Area improvement	Is the area cleaner than before the scheme was in place?	▪ Brief questionnaire to users. ▪ Number of waste piles before and after the scheme.
Convenience	Is the scheme convenient to use, i.e. times of collection, placement of waste for collection?	▪ Brief questionnaire to users. ▪ Study of responsibilities of users regarding scheme.
Affordability	Is the scheme affordable to all? Does the service represent good value for money?	▪ Questionnaire to users. ▪ How many people actually pay for the service on a regular basis? ▪ Survey of income levels of community.
Frequency and reliability	Is the service of reasonable frequency and reliability?	▪ Brief survey of users regarding satisfaction with frequency and reliability of service. ▪ Number of missing days or breakdowns when service was not available. ▪ Survey of times at which waste is collected from householders (say over one month).
Extra waste	Is there a system available to take care of extra waste generated during festivals etc.? Is there a service to remove construction debris?	▪ Brief questionnaire to users if this service is provided and how well it is provided. ▪ Check with the service provider. ▪ Survey of un-collected piles of extra waste in the area.
Increase in rental and land values	Have the users experienced other effects of the scheme, e.g. an increase in rental and land values?	▪ Questionnaire to users. ▪ Check details with estate agents and landlords.
Complaints system	Is there an efficient complaints procedure in place? What is the response system and are people prepared to complain if they feel it is necessary?	▪ Research complaints and response systems. ▪ Ask users whether they know how to make complaints and whether they would/do complain.
Sustainability	Is the scheme sustainable?	▪ Survey the payments/costs of the scheme. ▪ Survey of any problems experienced so far — Can these be overcome?

1.3.2   The municipality's perspective

How does the municipality judge the scheme?

Table 2. The municipality's perspective

Indicator	Description	Means to measure
Area improvement	Is the area cleaner than before the scheme was in place?	■ Brief questionnaire to users. ■ Number of waste piles before and after the scheme.
Municipal support	How much support does the municipality have to give the scheme? Do the results represent good value from these inputs?	■ Questionnaire to municipality on quantity and nature of inputs and value of results.
Impact on municipal services	Are municipal workers diverted from their proper jobs? Does the scheme take pressure off the municipal services? Has the scheme assisted the municipality to increase its capacity in solid waste activities?	■ Survey of municipal workers on activities done in their work time. ■ Survey of effects on secondary collection stage (Is there enhanced pressure to ensure this service is provided frequently? Is there more waste for transportation?). ■ Survey of any new developments that have taken place since the inception of the scheme. ■ Questionnaire to municipality regarding capacity building.
Staff satisfaction	Are municipal staff satisfied with the scheme?	■ Question municipal staff regarding satisfaction. ■ Monitor complaints about the scheme from municipal staff.
Complaints	Has the scheme resulted in a reduction in the number of complaints received by the municipality regarding waste collection?	■ Survey of number, intensity and nature of complaints.

1.3.3 The NGO's perspective

How does the NGO judge the scheme?

In this case, considering NGO who is involved in promoting primary solid waste collection schemes, may include supplying equipment, micro-credit etc.

Table 3. The NGO's perspective		
Indicator	*Description*	*Means to measure*
Replicability	Does the scheme provide a replicable model for further projects?	■ Brief questionnaire to NGO regarding replicability of the scheme. ■ Survey of pertinent aspects of the scheme and the scheme area that affect replicability.
Sustainability	Will the scheme be sustained once all assistance from the NGO is withdrawn?	■ Survey the payments/costs of the scheme. ■ Survey of any problems experienced so far — Can these be overcome? ■ Survey of the amount and nature of support presently supplied by the NGO.
Area improvement	Is the area cleaner than before the scheme was in place?	■ Brief questionnaire to users. ■ Number of waste piles before and after the scheme.
Fulfillment of specific aims	Has the scheme fulfilled other aims, for example, creation of livelihoods, improvement in health etc.?	■ Questionnaire to NGO regarding aims of scheme. ■ Surveys based on evaluating achievement of aims.

1.3.4 The CBO's perspective

How does the CBO judge the scheme?

In this case, considering a CBO who acts as initiator to the inception of primary collection scheme.

Table 4. The CBO's perspective		
Indicator	*Description*	*Means to measure*
User satisfaction	Are the users satisfied with the scheme?	■ Survey of number, intensity and nature of complaints.
Area improvement	Is the area cleaner than before the scheme was in place?	■ Brief questionnaire to users. ■ Number of waste piles before and after the scheme.
Sustainability	Will the scheme be sustained?	■ Survey the payments/costs of the scheme. ■ Survey of any problems experienced so far — Can these be overcome?
Recognition	Do the users recognize that the scheme is in place due to the efforts of the CBO?	■ Questionnaire to users to see if they believe the CBO plays an essential role in the successful scheme.

1.3.5 The local politician's perspective

How do the local politicians judge the scheme?

Table 5. The local politician's perspective		
Indicator	*Description*	*Means to measure*
Area improvement	Is the area cleaner than before the scheme was in place?	■ Brief questionnaire to users. ■ Number of waste piles before and after the scheme.
Replicability	Does the scheme provide a replicable model for further projects?	■ Brief questionnaire to operator regarding replicability of the scheme. ■ Survey of pertinent aspects of the scheme and the scheme area that affect replicability.
Recognition	Do the users recognize that the scheme is in place due to the efforts of the local politicians?	■ Questionnaire to users to see if they believe the local politician plays an essential role in the successful scheme. ■ Questionnaire to users to see if the scheme has increased the popularity of the local politician.

1.3.6   The small contractor's perspective

How do the small contractors judge the scheme?

In this case, considering small contractors who use their entrepreneurial initiative to undertake to provide a primary collection scheme.

Table 6. The small contractor's perspective		
Indicator	**Description**	**Means to measure**
Sustainability	Will the scheme be sustained?	▪ Survey the payments/costs of the scheme. ▪ Survey of any problems experienced so far — Can these be overcome?
Sustainable livelihood	Has the scheme resulted in the creation of a sustainable livelihood for the small contractor?	▪ Measure income of small contractor compared to before the scheme.
User satisfaction	Are the users satisfied with the scheme?	▪ Survey of number, intensity and nature of complaints.
Recognition	Do the users recognize that the system is in place due to the efforts of the small contractors?	▪ Questionnaire to users to see if they believe that the small contractors play an essential role in the successful scheme.

1.3.7   The sweeper's perspective

How do the sweepers judge the scheme?

In this case, considering municipally employed sweepers who also undertake primary collection as part of a supplementary scheme.

Table 7. The sweeper's perspective		
Indicator	**Description**	**Means to measure**
Increased income	Has the scheme resulted in an increased income for the sweeper?	▪ Assess the sweepers income before and after the inception of the project.
Recognition	Do the users of the scheme realize that is in place due to the efforts of the sweepers? Has this increased their respect for sweepers?	▪ Questionnaire to users whether they know that the scheme is in place due to the efforts of sweepers and whether this has changed their opinion of sweepers.
Problems with the municipality	Has participation in the scheme resulted in problems between the sweeper and the municipality?	▪ Question sweepers and their municipal supervisors.

1.4   Repetition of indicators

Some indicators are important from more than one perspective. For example, an increase in the cleanliness of the area is not only important to the local residents (users) but also the municipality, the NGO, the local elected representative etc. When this occurs, it is important that they are included in more than one table in order that it is remembered that the particular factor is an issue for each of the stakeholders.

1.5   Guidelines for use of these indicators

These indicators have been prepared for use by fieldworkers when assessing primary collection schemes. It is intended that they be used as a checklist during the formulation of assessment activities. The final choice of methods and other details are left to the fieldworkers who must choose it on the basis of local knowledge. In some cases, it may be appropriate to develop questionnaires or interviews with the various stakeholders. In this case, they can be developed around the indicator list. In other circumstances, it may be possible to formulate focus group meetings or conduct work surveys. In each case, it is intended that the indicators can provide guidance on the main issues that must be addressed.

There are also many issues that should be considered in any research project.

- **Size of sample group.** The groups used to gather information must be of a representative size to the total population involved in the scheme. It may be aimed to find out the views of a sample group, which constitute 5% of the total population, but the group should not consist of less than 30 people.

- **Selection of sample group.** The sample group should be representative of the population and be gathered from a cross section of socio-economic groups present in the area. The indicators help to ensure that each main group of stakeholders is considered but each group will have many sub-sections. For example, the users may be from both high-income areas and low-income areas. It is important to think about how the individual participants are chosen. For example, in many cases, the easiest way to find willing participants is with the help of the organization who runs the primary collection scheme. However, the people chosen will, most likely, be previously known to the organization and hence be more likely to know about and support the scheme.

- **The research method used.** There are many different methods that can be used to gather information such as independent interviews, group discussion, focus groups, work surveys etc. The method used should be selected carefully by the fieldworker depending on the local situation, the time and resources available etc. Although questionnaires/interviews have been suggested as the 'means to measure' for many of these indicators, they do not always yield the most accurate results. Often, more meaningful data can be gathered by group discussion, focus groups etc. In each case, special consideration must be given to the wording of questions etc. The 'description' of each indicator is not intended to be a question for use in interview but merely an aid for the reader.

■ **Qualitative information.** The above information must be triangulated by qualitative surveys, open-ended discussions, observations etc., in order to crosscheck the findings and reach definite conclusions.

Khulna City

NEPAL

Brahmaputra

Rangpur

INDIA

Jamuna

Mymensingh

Ganges

Rājshāhi

Padma

DHAKA

Nārāyanganj

Chāndpur

INDIA

Khulna

Barisāl

Mongla Port
(Chālna Port)

Chittagong

Mouths of the Ganges

Cox's
Bāzār

BURMA

| 0 | 50 | 100 km |
| 0 | 50 | 100 mi |

Bay of Bengal

Source: CIA, 2000

2.

Case Study: Khulna City

Khulna City is situated in Khulna District, in the southwestern area of Bangladesh in the Ganges delta. It is the third largest city in Bangladesh, with an estimated population of 1.2 million (2000) and a population growth rate of 5% per year. It is a river port and the trade and processing centre for the products of the Sundarbans, a swampy, forested coastal region. Agricultural products are processed, especially rice, oilseed and cotton. There are also industries in wood processing and shipbuilding.

The city occupies an area of approximately 267sq km. The city core is about a quarter of the total city area and is densely populated. It has mostly multi-storied residential and commercial buildings. The rest of the city is a mixture of urban and peri-urban areas. There are several low-income areas and slums throughout the city.

2.1 Solid waste management in Khulna

As with many major cities in developing countries, Khulna is experiencing huge problems in dealing with the solid waste generated in the city every day. A fast growing population, coupled with an increase in industrial activities and uncontrolled urbanization, has lead to rapidly increasing quantities of waste being generated. Using an estimated generation rate of 0.2kg/household/day it can be calculated that approximately 240 tons of solid waste is generated in Khulna City everyday (Murtaza and Rahman, 2000). However, only 60 (Chowdhury, 2000) to 120 tons (Monsoor, 2000) of the generated waste is collected daily by KCC and reaches the municipal disposal site. Therefore, between 120 and 180 tons of waste remains uncollected every day (estimate between $\frac{1}{2}$ and $\frac{1}{3}$). Some of this is recycled by the informal recycling industries that exist in the area. The remaining uncollected waste is often dumped in an uncontrolled manner throughout the city, clogging drains, blocking roads and occupying vacant plots of land. This not only causes problems of flooding and increased traffic congestion but also presents a health risk to the local communities.

Khulna City Corporation is responsible for the operation and maintenance of municipal services including solid waste management. The City Corporation is headed by an elected Mayor and operates through 41 elected Ward Commissioners, one for each of the 31 Wards and an additional 10 women Ward Commissioners. It is made up of eight functional departments (e.g. administration, engineering and conservancy). The conservancy department is responsible for solid waste management, street sweeping, public latrines and urinals, cleaning of drains, etc. The solid waste management services comprise of the collection of waste from approximately 1,200 masonry bins, constructed by the City Corporation, located on roadsides throughout the city. Households are expected to dispose of their waste in the masonry bins. The waste is then transported to its final disposal site (approximately 8km from the city) by the City Corporation's trucks.

The City Corporation has recently acquired 10 demountable containers which are placed in prime collection points throughout the city.

According to the City Corporation, the problem of solid waste management is too extensive for them to manage. The conservancy tax (4% of holding tax) is not even sufficient to fund the level of service currently provided. For example, in 1998, funding from the tax was only Taka 2.7 million (1 US$ ≈ Taka 50), whereas the total expenditure by the conservancy department in that year was Taka 17.8 million. Thus, the City Corporation has to depend heavily on grants from the central government.

As a result of the poor service provided by the KCC, many NGOs, CBOs and private organizations have developed solid waste management projects. These projects have developed in order to assist the KCC in its waste management tasks. The main service provided by these groups is primary collection of waste.

2.2 The solid waste management project

The main objective of this project was to improve the solid waste management systems operating in the area, in order that a cleaner, more hygienic environment be developed. A vital aspect of the project was to increase community awareness and participation. The main activity of the project is the primary collection of solid waste from project areas. The project was financed by the Swiss Agency for Development and Co-operation (SDC), with technical and management support from the Water and Sanitation Programme (WSP). Prodipan, a Bangladesh-based NGO, currently operating in seven cities throughout the country, were selected to implement a three-year pilot project in solid waste management. This has led to a great reduction in the amount of waste that lines the streets. At present, these activities are still operated and managed by Prodipan, however, local communities are currently being prepared to take over these activities when Prodipan withdraws its support at the end of the three-year project period in December 2000.

The primary collection services currently operate in six wards serving 22 communities (or collection blocks), each of between 400 and 500 households, every day of the year (in total approximately 71,500 beneficiaries). The waste is collected from the households and disposed at a secondary disposal or transfer point. From here, the waste is collected by the KCC and taken to the final disposal point.

Prodipan have also been involved in community motivation and awareness raising activities, such as poster printing and billboard installation and training. Throughout the project period, various other problems have developed or become apparent to Prodipan. Where possible, steps have been made to attempt to solve these problems, often on a pilot project basis. For example, the development of improved waste transfer stations and an improvement in clinical waste management systems.

2.3   Communities studied

The particular community studied in this research was Maulivipara community in Ward 27. The community is a diverse mixture of both high- and low-income areas, slums positioned in between up-market properties. It was, therefore, possible to get the views of both high- and low-income households within the same community.

2.4   Methods used in fieldwork

Fieldwork was carried out with the help of Monir Chowdhury, the Prodipan Project Co-ordinator. He gave a good overview of the project activities by various visits and also assisted in more specific research tasks. He helped to select participants and organize the interviews with help from the local community organizers. He also acted as an interpreter throughout.

Interviews were carried out in a traditional manner with participants answering questions. These questions also acted as the basis for further discussion where appropriate. In most cases, interviews were carried out with each participant individually. However, it was felt that when interviewing the drivers and collectors, it would be desirable to interview both drivers and then both collectors simultaneously. This was done both due to time constraints and in the hope that some discussion may be prompted. It was also thought that the boys who were collectors might feel intimidated if they had to do the interviews individually.

Information was also gathered in a group discussion at the monthly meeting of Prodipan Community Organizers. This discussion mainly focused on problems that they had encountered in their communities but also touched on complaints that they had received.

2.5   Outcomes of fieldwork

The interviews and discussions were carried out both for the purpose of improving documentation of the Prodipan schemes and the assessment of these indicators.

2.5.1   The users' perspective

Interviews were carried out with users of the Prodipan primary collection scheme. Key informants were chosen, one from a high-income community and one from a low-income community. If more time were available, it would be advisable to interview a greater selection of users from a wider variety of socio-economic groups.

2.5.1.1   The high-income users' perspective

Table 8. The high-income users' perspective		
Indicator	**Description**	**Outcome**
Area improvement	Is the area cleaner than before the scheme was in place?	Yes, the area is now much cleaner. Initially the situation was very bad, waste was dumped in the streets and blocked the drains.
Convenience	Is the scheme convenient to use, i.e. times of collection, placement of waste for collection?	Yes, the service is convenient. The construction of a bin in the yard of our residential block has made the system more convenient, as we don't have to be in to hand over waste when the collector comes.
Affordability	Is the scheme affordable to all? Does the service represent good value for money?	Yes, she thinks that the scheme is affordable to all as there are different service charges for different income levels. She feels that the charges are very low and thinks that it is good value for money. She would be willing to increase her contribution if it meant the scheme could continue.
Frequency and reliability	Is the service of reasonable frequency and reliability?	Yes, waste is collected once a day. The service provided is excellent and the collectors are always on time.
Extra waste	Is there a system available to take care of extra waste generated during festivals etc.?	Normally the workers are given the day of Eid off, but to makeup for the missed day they do two collections the following day. This is sufficient to cope with the extra waste.
Increase in rental and land values	Have the users experienced other effects of the scheme, e.g. an increase in rental and land values?	She said that she did not know of any indirect benefits of the scheme and that she didn't really analyze things like that.
Complaints system	Is there an efficient complaints procedure in place? What is the response system and are people prepared to complain if they feel it is necessary?	Yes, she knows how to make a complaint about the service and would be prepared to complain if she felt that the system was not working.
Sustainability	Is the scheme sustainable?	If Prodipan withdraw support, she is not sure whether the community will be able to sustain the project. However, she stated that if Prodipan help the community to develop institutional and organizational skills, then the scheme could be sustained. She said that the people would want the scheme to continue, as they understand that the project helps them. She also said that she thought that people would be prepared to pay more for the service if necessary.

2.5.1.2   The low-income users' perspective

Table 9. The low-income users' perspective		
Indicator	**Description**	**Outcome**
Area improvement	Is the area cleaner than before the scheme was in place?	Yes, the area is cleaner than before the project was started. However, she doesn't know if it is cleaner than areas that don't have the scheme because all her Ward is covered and she rarely goes out of the Ward.
Convenience	Is the scheme convenient to use, i.e. times of collection, placement of waste for collection?	Yes, the system is convenient. The timing is particularly good as it normally means that most of the waste from the preparation of lunch is taken away almost as soon as it is generated. Even if the collectors are early, they only have the waste for 24 hours.
Affordability	Is the scheme affordable to all? Does the service represent good value for money?	The scheme is affordable to all (she pays Tk2 per month). She feels that this is good value for money and would be willing to pay more if it meant that the scheme could continue.
Frequency and reliability	Is the service of reasonable frequency and reliability?	Yes, waste is collected every day between 12 and 12.30.
Extra waste	Is there a system available to take care of extra waste generated during festivals etc.?	Yes, the communal bin provided is large enough to hold the extra waste generated, despite the fact that the collectors have Eid day off. The waste is then collected in the two collections that occur on the day that follows Eid.
Increase in rental and land values	Have the users experienced other effects of the scheme, e.g. an increase in rental and land values?	No awareness of indirect benefits.
Complaints system	Is there an efficient complaints procedure in place? What is the response system and are people prepared to complain if they feel it is necessary?	Yes, she knows how to make a complaint; there are many different ways she can choose, as she has a lot of contact with the Community Organizer. She has complained before.
Sustainability	Is the scheme sustainable?	Not sure how it would work if Prodipan withdrew its support. However, she is confident that it would continue (public support) as the Ward Commissioner will not let it stop.

2.5.2 The municipality's perspective

An interview was carried out with Fazl Abu Monsoor, Chief Executive Officer (CEO) of Khulna City Corporation (KCC).

Table 10. The municipality's perspective		
Indicator	**Description**	**Outcome**
Area improvement	Is the area cleaner than before the scheme was in place?	Yes. Prior to the intervention waste was dumped everywhere, in drains etc. Now householders don't dump waste indiscriminately and KCC is now able to collect more waste.
Municipal support	How much support does the municipality give the scheme? Do the results represent good value from these inputs?	The municipality supports the scheme by giving them official permission to collect waste in these areas and ensuring the waste is collected effectively from the new transfer points. The KCC and Prodipan have a good working relationship. KCC have stated that if more communities wish to have primary collection schemes and are willing to finance and run these (CBOs), then KCC will provide the rickshaw van.
Impact on municipal services	How are municipal services affected?	Has not affected the municipal sweepers as they were not involved in primary collection and are still not involved. However, their job has been made easier as less waste dumped around the place, but still same number employed. However, the sweepers do not realize that their job has been made easier.
		KCC has expanded its secondary collection capacity by purchasing more vans and employing more staff. They have also purchased 10 demountable containers.
Staff satisfaction	Are the municipal staff satisfied with the scheme?	Initially, there was opposition from sweepers as they thought that Prodipan were taking their jobs. Now they see that their jobs still exist, so they are pleased with the schemes.
		The CEO seems pleased as it has resulted in an improvement of SWM without great inputs from him — he is pleased that Prodipan are taking up clinical waste collection as the prime minister suggested it to him!
Complaints	Has the scheme resulted in a reduction in the number of complaints received by KCC regarding SWM?	The KCC does not operate a formal system of complaints, but there was a general feeling that they have reduced.

2.5.3   The NGO's perspective

An interview was carried out with Monir Alam Chowdhury, the Project Co-ordinator of the Municipal Solid Waste Management Project for Prodipan. Some of the indicators were also discussed during field visits.

Table 11. The NGO's perspective		
Indicator	*Description*	*Outcome*
Replicability	Does the scheme provide a replicable model for further projects?	Yes, Prodipan chose a cross section of socio-economic areas to make the project more useful as a pilot project. The schemes have already been replicated but in some cases with limited effect (they have run into financial and management problems).
Sustainability	Will the scheme be sustained once all assistance from the NGO is withdrawn?	He feels that the project will continue when support from Prodipan is withdrawn. Some primary collection blocks are already nearly financially sustainable (Tk3000 per month). Prodipan are training communities to be able to have the ability to continue the schemes.
Area improvement	Is the area cleaner than before the scheme was in place?	Yes, the area is much cleaner.
Fulfillment of specific aims	Has the scheme fulfilled other aims, for example, creation of livelihoods, improvement in health etc.?	Aims were to establish community-based solid waste management in a sustainable manner, where the community will be empowered to run the programme in a financially sustainable manner. He feels that they are on target to fulfill these aims and is confident that, given time, it will happen in all areas.

2.5.4   The local elected representative's perspective

During the time spent in Khulna, the local elected representative (Ward Commissioner) was not available for comment. However, discussions with both Prodipan and the local communities suggest that the Ward Commissioner supported the primary collection schemes whole-heartedly. The low-income users suggested that the scheme would be sustainable because the Ward Commissioner would not let the scheme fold.

2.5.5 The worker's perspective

Whilst carrying out the research in Khulna, it became apparent that one important group of people was not explicitly included in the Success and Sustainability Indicators, even though they could have a large impact on the schemes. This group was the workers who actually carry out the primary collection. The reason that this group was not initially included was due to the fact that the indicators intend to be suitable for all systems of organizations of primary collection schemes. In cases where primary collection was operated by an NGO, it was perceived that the workers' views would be included in the views of the NGO. However, it became apparent in the case study area, that in fact the NGO and the workers formed two very distinct and different groups. It was highly likely that their views would differ considerably. The workers could have a large impact on the success and sustainability of such a scheme, as, in the end, it is these people that give the service. If they do not think it worthwhile or do not think that they are paid enough, they may not carry out their work effectively and hence the scheme may fail.

2.5.5.1 The drivers' perspective

Interviews were carried out with two drivers. Outlined below is a summary of the outcomes of both of their answers.

Table 12. The drivers' perspective		
Indicator	**Description**	**Outcome**
Job satisfaction	Are they satisfied with the job? Would they like to continue to do it?	Yes, they are satisfied with their jobs and would like to continue. They think that the job is worthwhile and that they are doing something good for the community.
Renumeration	Are they satisfied with the payment that they receive?	They are satisfied with the payment that they receive; in both cases it is more per hour than in their previous jobs.
Problems	What problems do they face in their job?	They have very few problems in their job. Occasionally, people complain about the collection time and there are other small complaints. When they started the job at the start of the scheme, they faced more opposition.
Perks	What extra perks do they receive?	They both pick valuable items from the waste, such as steel, and sell it to supplement their income. They also like the fact that they do not have to work all day and, so, have time for other activities and jobs.
Sustainability	Do they feel that the scheme is sustainable in the long-term?	—

2.5.5.2   *The collectors' perspective*

The interviews with collectors were also carried out simultaneously with two different collectors.

Table 13. The collectors' perspective		
Indicator	*Description*	*Outcome*
Job satisfaction	Are they satisfied with the job? Would they like to continue to do it?	They are satisfied with their jobs and would like to continue.
Renumeration	Are they satisfied with the payment that they receive?	Yes, they are satisfied with the payment that they get.
Problems	What problems do they face in their job?	They face very few problems throughout the day. Occasionally, they have problems with the way in which people store the waste or people making complaints.
Perks	What extra perks do they receive?	They receive free schooling. The hours of the job allow them to carry on (/start) schooling and Prodipan pay for this. They also make money from selling valuable waste.
Sustainability	Do they feel that the scheme is sustainable in the long-term?	—

3.

Conclusions

3.1 An assessment of the success and sustainability indicators

The results obtained from this study seem to show that the 'Success and Sustainability' indicators are reasonably useful in assessing a primary collection scheme. The information was mainly quick and easy to collect through interviews and the information gained was relevant to the specific indicator to be assessed.

There is only one indicator whose usefulness has been brought into question by this study, that of the indirect benefits of the scheme, such as a rise in land prices and a reduction in health problems. In this case, it was found that many members of the community lacked a clear understanding of links between the primary collection scheme and the indirect benefits. Where an awareness of the links between these benefits and the collection schemes does not exist, such benefits will have little influence on the success or sustainability of the scheme from the community perspective. However, they may be used as an indicator by which the NGO or municipality judge the scheme. For example, the municipality may find that the scheme has led to fewer illnesses amongst the communities and hence a reduction in workdays lost due to illness (and hence be of economic benefit to the city).

This study has also led to suggestions of how to improve the indicators by including a few extra features. The main adjustment that has been recommended is the inclusion of an extra section for the views of the workers employed in the scheme. (The reason for this is outlined in the 'Outcomes' section of this document.)

The study has drawn attention to a further aspect of primary collection schemes that may affect their success and sustainability. This is particularly relevant to schemes that are initially run by NGOs with the intention that, after some time, support from the initiator is withdrawn and they are taken over by the local community. In this case, it is important that a well-defined withdrawal plan has been developed before the scheme is started. One should look carefully at any of the aspects of the scheme that may not be sustainable if run solely by the communities, and examine any strategies to prepare the community to manage such projects. In the case study scheme, it is noted that Prodipan included members of the community in the running of the primary collection service by initiating Environmental Development Committees. However, one should also be aware of other factors that may not be sustainable when run by the communities. For example, Prodipan have provided their workers with many perks, such as uniforms, refreshments and schooling. These perks represent extra cost to the local communities and hence the need to collect a higher service charge. If these perks are simply withdrawn with the withdrawal of support from the NGO, the workers may become disenchanted with the scheme. If the communities attempt to continue to provide the workers with these benefits, they may have more difficulty becoming financially sustainable or there may be opposition from the members of the community. In order to be able to assess the usefulness of this as an indicator more fully, further research needs to be done.

3.2   Limitations of this study / Suggestions for further study

There are several limitations of this study that should be considered when assessing the validity of the results. These are outlined below:

- This scheme seems to be running very well, so it is difficult to make an assessment as to how crucial each indicator is to the success and sustainability of the project. In order to investigate this, it would be necessary to spend some time investigating schemes that have failed or are failing and assess them using the indicators. It may be discovered that the reason for failure is not included as an indicator. It would also be necessary to investigate several successful schemes to find out whether any of the outcomes of the indicators give surprising results. It may be the case that a scheme is sustainable, even though several of the indicators seem to point to a failing scheme.

- Due to time limitations, this study only uses interviews with the major stakeholders to assess the indicators. In order for a more extensive assessment of these indicators, it is important to also assess the other methods suggested, such as surveys. Further study should be made into the ease and applicability of these methods of measuring the indicators.

- This study only involved the use of one case study. In order to get a fuller picture of the use and applicability of these indicators, it is necessary to study a wide variety of primary collection schemes, for example, one run by a micro-enterprise, one run by a community-based organization etc. It is only through the use of these indicators in more varied circumstances that more problems will be highlighted and improvements can be made.

- Due to a lack of time and local knowledge, the interviews carried out in this study were arranged by the NGO who run the scheme. This may have resulted in a biased sample due to the fact that these community members were known by the NGO and so may have had a higher awareness of the scheme than an average member of the community.

3.3 Overall conclusions

This study has sought to field-test the success and sustainability indicators for primary solid waste collection systems, as prepared by the project team as part of the Knowledge and Research (KAR) project, *Capacity Building for Primary Collection of Solid Waste*. It has been found that these indicators are a valuable resource for those planning research involved in this research field. They provide a useful checklist for the fieldworker but, in each case, full consideration must be given into the methods chosen to gather information.

This research has lead to small changes in the indicator list and a revised list can be found in Appendix 1. This list of indicators is not thought to be comprehensive for all projects and it is envisaged that adjustments will continue to be made as the list is used. Use on further, more diverse projects is likely to result in the addition of more indicators and possibly the subtraction of others.

Whilst undertaking this study, it became apparent that it would be appropriate to publish a list of guidelines for use of these indicators. These guidelines have been developed and can be found in Section 1.4.

References

Chowdhury, M. (2000) (Project Co-ordinator Municipal Solid Waste Management Project (MSWMP), Prodipan, Khulna, Bangladesh). Personal Communication.

Monsoor, F.A. (2000) (Chief Executive Officer, Khulna City Corporation, Khulna, Bangladesh). Personal Communication (Interview).

Murtaza, G. and Rahman, A. (1999) *Solid Waste Management in Khulna City and a Case Study of a CBO: Amader Paribartan*. Bangladesh.

CIA (2000) http://www.odci.gov/cia/publications/factbook/bg.html

Bibliography

Coad, A. (1999) *Improving municipal solid waste management in Khulna*. WSP Programme, Bangladesh.

Murtaza, G. and Rahman, A. (1999) *Solid Waste Management in Khulna City and a Case Study of a CBO: Amader Paribartan*. Bangladesh.

Narayan, D. (1993) *Participatory evaluation — Tools for managing change in water and sanitation*. World Bank Technical Paper No. 207, World Bank, Washington D.C.

Pratt, B. and Loizos, P. (1992) *Choosing research methods — Data collection for development workers*. Development Guidelines No. 7, Oxfam.

Prodipan, (1999) *Activity Report on Municipal Solid Waste Management Project, Prodipan, Khulna. July '99 – December '99*. Prodipan.

Appendix 1.

The Revised Success and Sustainability Indicators

The users' perspective

How do the users judge the scheme?

Table 14. The users' perspective		
Indicator	**Description**	**Means to measure**
Area improvement	Is the area cleaner than before the scheme was in place?	■ Brief questionnaire to users. ■ Number of waste piles before and after the scheme.
Convenience	Is the scheme convenient to use, i.e. times of collection, placement of waste for collection?	■ Brief questionnaire to users. ■ Study of responsibilities of users regarding scheme.
Affordability	Is the scheme affordable to all? Does the service represent good value for money?	■ Questionnaire to users. ■ How many people actually pay for the service on a regular basis? ■ Survey of income levels of community.
Frequency and reliability	Is the service of reasonable frequency and reliability?	■ Brief survey of users regarding satisfaction with frequency and reliability of service. ■ Number of missing days or breakdowns when service was not available. ■ Survey of times at which waste is collected from householders (say over one month).
Extra waste	Is there a system available to take care of extra waste generated during festivals etc.? Is there a service to remove construction debris?	■ Brief questionnaire to users if this service is provided and how well it is provided. ■ Check with the service provider. ■ Survey of un-collected piles of extra waste in the area.
Complaints system	Is there an efficient complaints procedure in place? What is the response system and are people prepared to complain if they feel it is necessary?	■ Research complaints and response systems. ■ Ask users whether they know how to make complaints and whether they would/do complain.
Sustainability	Is the scheme sustainable?	■ Survey the payments/costs of the scheme. ■ Survey of any problems experienced so far — Can these be overcome?

The municipality's perspective

How does the municipality judge the scheme?

Table 15. The municipality's perspective		
Indicator	*Description*	*Means to measure*
Area improvement	Is the area cleaner than before the scheme was in place?	■ Brief questionnaire to users. ■ Number of waste piles before and after the scheme.
Municipal support	How much support does the municipality have to give the scheme? Do the results represent good value from these inputs?	■ Questionnaire to municipality on quantity and nature of inputs and value of results.
Impact on municipal services	Are municipal workers diverted from their proper jobs? Does the scheme take pressure off the municipal services? Has the scheme assisted the municipality to increase its capacity in solid waste activities?	■ Survey of municipal workers on activities done in their work time. ■ Survey of effects on secondary collection stage (Is there enhanced pressure to ensure this service is provided frequently? Is there more waste for transportation?). ■ Survey of any new developments that have taken place since the inception of the scheme. ■ Questionnaire to municipality regarding capacity building.
Staff satisfaction	Are municipal staff satisfied with the scheme?	■ Question municipal staff regarding satisfaction. ■ Monitor complaints about the scheme from municipal staff.
Complaints	Has the scheme resulted in a reduction in the number of complaints received by the municipality regarding waste collection?	■ Survey of number, intensity and nature of complaints.

The NGO's perspective

How does the NGO judge the scheme?

In this case, considering NGO who is involved in promoting primary solid waste collection schemes, may include supplying equipment, micro-credit etc.

Table 16. The NGO's perspective		
Indicator	*Description*	*Means to measure*
Replicability	Does the scheme provide a replicable model for further projects?	■ Brief questionnaire to NGO regarding replicability of the scheme. ■ Survey of pertinent aspects of the scheme and the scheme area that affect replicability.
Sustainability	Will the scheme be sustained once all assistance from the NGO is withdrawn ? Is there a well-defined withdrawal plan?	■ Survey the payments/costs of the scheme. ■ Survey of any problems experienced so far — Can these be overcome? ■ Survey of the amount and nature of support presently supplied by the NGO. ■ Investigate the plans for support withdrawal.
Area improvement	Is the area cleaner than before the scheme was in place?	■ Brief questionnaire to users. ■ Number of waste piles before and after the scheme.
Fulfillment of specific aims	Has the scheme fulfilled other aims, for example, creation of livelihoods, improvement in health etc.?	■ Questionnaire to NGO regarding aims of scheme. ■ Surveys based on evaluating achievement of aims.

The CBO's perspective

How does the CBO judge the scheme?

In this case, considering a CBO who acts as initiator to the inception of primary collection scheme.

Table 17. The CBO's perspective		
Indicator	*Description*	*Means to measure*
User satisfaction	Are the users satisfied with the scheme?	▪ Survey of number, intensity and nature of complaints.
Area improvement	Is the area cleaner than before the scheme was in place?	▪ Brief questionnaire to users. ▪ Number of waste piles before and after the scheme.
Sustainability	Will the scheme be sustained?	▪ Survey the payments/costs of the scheme. ▪ Survey of any problems experienced so far — Can these be overcome?
Recognition	Do the users recognize that the scheme is in place due to the efforts of the CBO?	▪ Questionnaire to users to see if they believe the CBO plays an essential role in the successful scheme.

The local politician's perspective

How do the local politicians judge the scheme?

Table 18. The local politician's perspective		
Indicator	*Description*	*Means to measure*
Area improvement	Is the area cleaner than before the scheme was in place?	▪ Brief questionnaire to users. ▪ Number of waste piles before and after the scheme.
Replicability	Does the scheme provide a replicable model for further projects?	▪ Brief questionnaire to operator regarding replicability of the scheme. ▪ Survey of pertinent aspects of the scheme and the scheme area that affect replicability.
Recognition	Do the users recognize that the scheme is in place due to the efforts of the local politicians?	▪ Questionnaire to users to see if they believe the local politician plays an essential role in the successful scheme. ▪ Questionnaire to users to see if the project has increased the popularity of the local politician.

The worker's perspective

How do the workers perceive the scheme?

Table 19. The worker's perspective		
Indicator	**Description**	**Means to measure**
Job satisfaction	Are they satisfied with the job? Would they like to continue to do it?	■ Questionnaire to workers. ■ Records of resignations from workers.
Renumeration	Are they satisfied with the payment that they receive?	■ Questionnaire to workers.
Problems	What problems do they face in their job?	■ Questionnaire to workers. ■ Survey of working practices/ problems encountered.
Perks	What extra perks do they receive?	■ Questionnaire to workers. ■ Survey of working practices.
Sustainability	Do they feel that the scheme is sustainable in the long-term?	■ Questionnaire to workers.

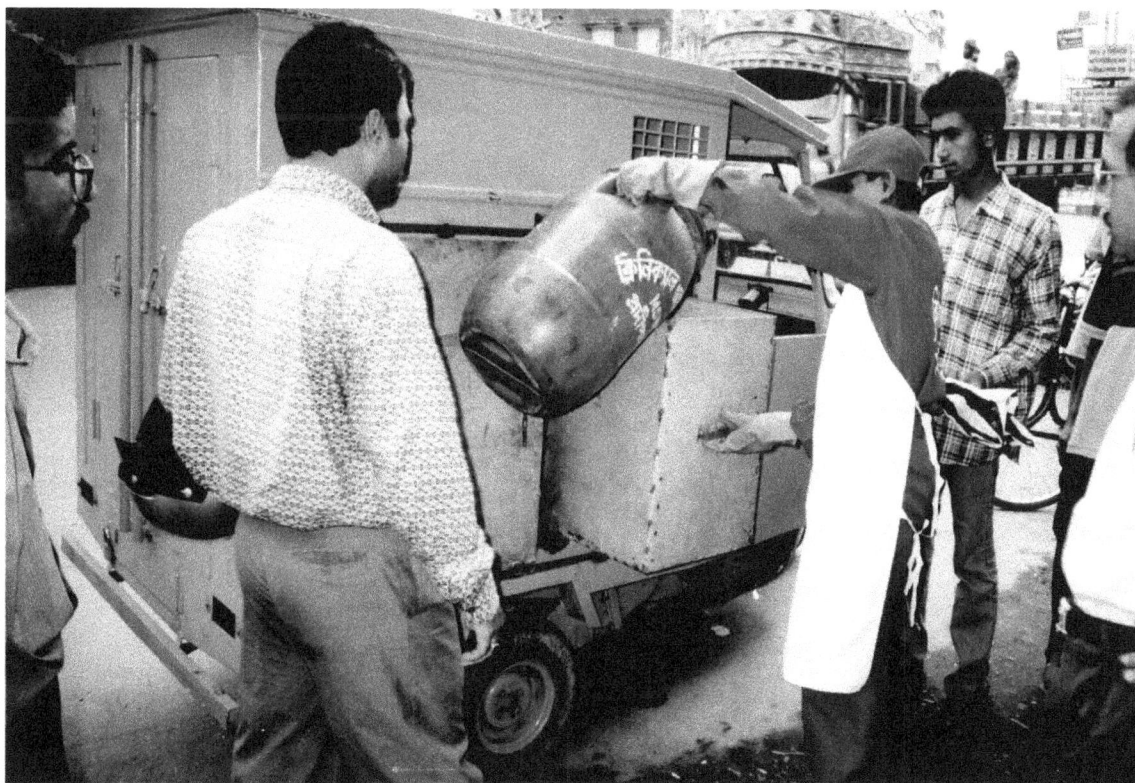

The small contractor's perspective

How do the small contractors judge the scheme?

In this case, considering small contractors who use their entrepreneurial initiative to undertake to provide a primary collection scheme.

Table 20. The small contractor's perspective		
Indicator	**Description**	**Means to measure**
Sustainability	Will the scheme be sustained?	■ Survey the payments/costs of the scheme. ■ Survey of any problems experienced so far — Can these be overcome?
Sustainable livelihood	Has the scheme resulted in the creation of a sustainable livelihood for the small contractor?	■ Measure income of small contractor compared to before the scheme.
User satisfaction	Does the small contractor receive lots of complaints from the users of the service?	■ Survey of number, intensity and nature of complaints.
Recognition	Do the users recognize that the system is in place due to the efforts of the small contractors?	■ Questionnaire to users to see if they believe that the small contractors play an essential role in the successful scheme.

The sweeper's perspective

How do the sweepers judge the scheme?

In this case, considering municipally employed sweepers who also undertake primary collection as part of a supplementary scheme.

Table 21. The sweeper's perspective		
Indicator	**Description**	**Means to measure**
Increased income	Has the scheme resulted in an increased income for the sweeper?	■ Assess the sweepers income before and after the inception of the project.
Recognition	Do the users of the scheme realize that is in place due to the efforts of the sweepers? Has this increased their respect for sweepers?	■ Questionnaire to users on whether they know that the scheme is in place due to the efforts of sweepers and whether this has changed their opinion of sweepers.
Problems with the municipality	Has participation in the scheme resulted in problems between the sweeper and the municipality?	■ Question sweepers and their municipal supervisors.

www.ingramcontent.com/pod-product-compliance
Lightning Source LLC
Chambersburg PA
CBHW080927050426
42334CB00055B/2831